The real MVP? Just call me AP

Alyssa Parker

BookLeaf Publishing

India | USA | UK

Presentation by *BookLeaf Publishing*

Web: www.bookleafpub.com

E-mail: info@bookleafpub.com

ISBN: 9789363314986

First edition 2024

Dedicated to my grandma Donna Wood, I never got to read your poems or meet you before you left this world but they tell me we are exactly alike. Which probably isn't a good thing, but I choose to take it as a compliment. I think of you often and wonder if we would have been close. I'm misunderstood just like you. I'm sorry you had to go but I just thought you should know… somebody out here finally understands your definition of lonely and I don't blame you. Until we get to meet, I know you stay watching over me 🖤

ACKNOWLEDGEMENT

To anyone who added to my growing list of trauma, Thanks so much, I turned that pain into a great story that can help others.

It's All About Precision

DHS search for bruises
Verbal abuse leaves no proof it's,
Just like me it's all useless
Nobody cares what your truth is
You went through hell came out truth less
You got problems and more excuses
Straight from the heart I got lyrics
You got rhymes nobody feelin
Take the cards you dealt, deal with it
You think my hand was better? We got different
dealers then
I'll flip the cards and the table still pull out a win
Don't got a mom but her Facebook got children
Upgraded from mom you a milf with some kids
Babysitter lackin my best interests
Forced to drink milk while they laugh and grin
Oh look we're watching A Bug's Life again
What if I wanted a hug? We don't play pretend
We play the victim and blame our friends
Gave up on trying to win
It's all about precision
Use that towel clean up messes I didn't make
Watch it all soak in
No second best I'm straight A's again
Just another day in the life of your kid

You teach for a living
Not a home just a house we living in
You're grown I'm irrelevant
Rub it in yeah we get it
Scrub the floors more Cinderella shit
No step kids or kids we all mixed in
Dinner on the stove propane gettin low
Paper towel soaked
The flames going up
Your words make me choke, I spit it up
That milk gettin old, expiration date comin up
No consolation prize, always the runner up
No parents I'm just a bug
Stay under your feet yeah I swept the rug
You wanna connect I said "where's the plug"
Laugh it up stay calling me dumb
Said no "what ifs" sittin on your throne in your
kingdom
Postin sweet comments I get a thumbs up
Call me a mistake that's your fuck up
Gave me a broken ladder, said level up
Put up a fence it's a trick, but the electric it hums
Just like a bug you made me small enough
Flew right past while your nose was up
Electrocuted now that smoke comin from my
lungs
Fire stays within healing bruises that didn't need
no cover up
Just like that stove yeah I lit it up

That food and shelter didn't take care of us
You had the whole deck I still called your bluff
Dot the I's cross the T's, electric bill due your
time is up
We'll cross that bridge when DHS never comes

Utility Player

Don't Look in my eyes
Might get petrified
Basilisk moving through the pipes
Peter Piper picked the pickled peppers
Tongue twister so good taste it after
I'd say that's my good girl but she even better
Clean up my mess then she get wetter
Utility player I can do it all
Kill marry fuck just don't fall
Scar tissue that I wish you saw
Red Hot Chili Peppers kinda song
Half Angel half devil
Half healed half get on my level
Out of this world upside down kiss
Peter Parker to spider man, guess I got bit
Got the love bug now I'm starting to itch
Dr Jekyll you can't Hyde, somebody writin a
script
Ride or die but somebody lied
Right person at the wrong time
Bonnie and Clyde put Clyde to the side
French fries I'll take the number 5
Straight to the gut death punch, 3 fingers inside
She's comin, you goin, that girl is mine
😈

Close your eyes ima Marco Polo find
Shoot your shot swing away don't miss the signs
Aliens UFO we keep it on the low
Most things just for show
I was raised to the left cause that shit wasn't
right
My mind a little twisted bop it flick it
Now Cha cha slide
Just don't hit my blindside
Stay in your lane watch me pass by
Stayin out late I been up for days
Don't worry about me I'm good I'm great
Treat me like your kid I'll show you how I was
raised
Slightest hint of abandon I'd outdo you anyways
You ever been where the sun doesn't shine
Black out curtain only throwin shade
What would you do if I let in the light
If I'm your sunshine I prayed for the rain
Go back in time take the bullet from her brain
Scarecrow lion tin man the wizard is dead
No brain, courage, heart or head
Childhood trauma not a discussion or topic
Losing a parent wasn't enough universe said
"watch me top it"
Grieving a parent who still alive wish I had more
options
Switch up the angle I guess I'm grateful

Different environment different climate I thrive
in the chaos
I survived even after every loss
Resilient she thinks ima boss
Not sure what she sees
Some deep down version of me
She holds space for that little girl underneath
Like the light at the end of a tunnel nightmare
turned to day dream
Like the "haha" after reading a new meme
Like I wish you the best (but the best was
me 😆)
Can't hide, don't reach
Close your eyes count sheep

Is Love Supposed to Feel This Way?

Fuck
I messed it up again
I don't feel wrong for the things I feel
I don't feel right for sharing them either
I can't change my feelings
I don't like hiding them
What happens to us if I share them all?
You push me away
I overwhelmed you again
The things I feel for you are too much
Too heavy to process
Maybe you don't want to process
Maybe that's the scariest part of all
I read the poems you write for me
I think about the ring in your shopping cart that
I've never seen
I think about the song lyrics you always share
with me
I think about the way you look at me
I think about your smile and laugh far too often
Is this normal?
Is this okay..
Feelings are supposed to be okay
But mine have never been safe to share

I feel nothing but love
But all I bring is destruction
Maybe idk how to love the right way
I try
I put in the effort
I communicate
I give you the reassurance
I give you whatever you crave at the time
Then I end my nights alone
Am I allowed to crave you sometimes too?
I'm afraid it's more than sometimes
I'm afraid you consume me in ways I didn't
know possible
Almost like I can't breathe if you're too far
away for too long
Am I crazy for feeling this way..
Am I crazy for believing you felt it too?
Surrounded by narcissists really fucked with my
head
So many issues I still need to work through
I'm starting to love myself again
I'm starting to enjoy the quiet and the stillness
that comes with being alone
Feels like I'm sinking into a dark hole
Sometimes feels like I disappear completely
Would anybody actually notice..
Maybe for a little bit
But if my presence isn't craved then my absence
will eventually be forgotten

It'll be like I never existed
Maybe life would be easier for you that way
No. It would definitely be easier for you
Idk if you want me to stay or if you want me to
go
Idk if we want the same things or if I made it up
in my head
I think it was almost possible at one point
But I think you changed your mind somewhere
along the way
It's easier this way
I don't blame you
I've never blamed you for hurting me
Because I understand..
And I've always encouraged it
If it keeps you from being hurt
If it keeps you happy and safe
That's really all I want
I want you to have everything that you want in
life
I want you with me
But I can't say that over and over
I can't hope for that when it's not mutual
I can't lose sleep or lose my appetite again
trying to figure my thoughts out
I wish you would tell me how you feel
The raw and honest truth of it all
It would ease my mind in so many ways

It would reassure me that I didn't make this
crazy thing up in my head..
Is love supposed to feel this way?
Does it make you crazy?
I want to feel safe in your arms
I did for awhile
I still do on the days you're with me
I think you feel it too
But the guessing games have me going crazy
I just don't know..
Idk what I'm allowed to say or think or feel..
I just want to be me
I just want to learn to love you
Not in the ways that I personally want to love
you
But in all the ways that YOU need to be loved
I want you to feel a love that's selfless and easy
I want you to feel like you're coming home
Like you can breathe again
Like you matter at all times
Like you're worth it and always will be
Like you can be yourself
Like you're safe completely…
I'm still working on it
I promise
I'm never going to stop putting in the work
You deserve effort at all times
You deserve everything
Even if everything isn't me

I'll still be here
For whatever you need
I'll listen to all of your thoughts
I don't want to feel like I'm losing you
Like I'm losing us
Whatever we are (even the feelings you hide
from me)
Whatever we were
Whatever we're going to be..
It's all up in the air
Kinda like the moon
No expectations, just the thrill of the chase
Watching you shine your light on the world and
doing your thing
And choosing to love whatever face you show
that day
Whatever phase you're in
Whether you're hiding behind clouds or in plain
sight
You're beautiful to me all the same
Yeah..
I choose to love you like that
Unconditionally
No matter what the nights bring
No matter how long the days are without you
No matter how long it takes for you to come
back again
I know you'll come back
I know I'll see you again

Maybe in a different light
Maybe in a different time zone
Maybe in a different view that takes my breath
away all over again..
But I'll keep breathing
Because the simple fact of knowing I'll never
lose you
Is enough to get me through any day or night

S&A Combined

Houses are painted in black and white
No colors are allowed on display
Most kids learn how to separate the two
Lonely children mix theirs and call it grey

Narcissist who feels too little and an empath
who feels too much
Bring them together now there's a baby grey in
the bunch
4 years old thinking she might even be gay
Why would they love my rainbow when they
barely accepted my grey?

Refusing to see the real me, they stayed color
blind
Being raised not to see colors been fucking with
my mind
Why can't I show all the yellows and purples
and red?
Why limit my mind when they could expand
theirs instead??

Black and white means there's only right and
wrong
Should've been raised to be unique, independent
and strong..
It was always a choice between my colors or
them
Not allowed to have both, guess I'll marry a
"him"

Greys don't see things as simply right or simply
wrong
There's so many factors when it comes to people
getting along
This invisible leash holding me back been
starting to chafe
It's different with her, like my inner child finally
feels safe..

Everyone says they've got you but they don't
ever stay
She accepts all my colors, finds them beautiful
She even calls me Grey🩶

Forget Normal Dreams

Forget normal dreams, I got IT coming out the
faucet
Thought your girl was coming out? She still in
the closet
Never the manager just behind the scenes bossin
it
Oh that forbidden line? Yeah we stay crossin it

Had your number but I must've lost it
Maybe I'm lying, maybe I tossed it
Big talker when you're running the game
See who's left standing when you lose that fame

Let's play fair or maybe let's not?
I'll let ya know once I connect the dots
The writings on the wall blurring into bigger
pictures
I'd invite you along but you chose my sneak
dissers

Laugh it off it's no big deal!
Do it over again because it's not even real
The dictionary and I been tryna gain clarity
Is this totally normal or just insanity?

You think I believe in "for better or for worse?"
Reading the sky like it knows why I'm cursed
When's the right time to decide our own worth??
Think I'm slippery like liquid? Babe I been solid
since birth
Convince all these people to start demanding
better
You want them to care while you cryin in my
sweater?

Not even worried about the makeup stains
Fuck the dry clothes let's go dance in the rain
You funny like Jim Carrey or just starring on
Liar Liar?
Make those power moves baby, now you just
fired
You thought I baked pies but that's just my shit
Stay tuned to see what he finds next, me or the
clit

Keep that bedroom door locked with the secrets
inside
He hurt you again but you lettin it slide
99 lbs but still ridin the rides
You want the point? That's besides 💯

Forever Toning Down My Feelings

I hate that I love harder than most people
I'm forever toning down my feelings or keeping
my mouth shut when I have so many things I
want to say
For fear of pushing her away..
It's like the more I say the less words I receive
The more I care the more you don't care about
me
Once you know I'm hooked it's okay to leave
It's okay to treat me however because you know
you're not going to lose me
I feel like I'll never be treated the way I
deserve.. the way I treat her
Idk what's wrong with me
Why can't I just feel things at a normal level
A level where people don't take advantage of me
Why is loving someone so hard such a bad scary
thing
Why does it push her away
If she really loved me wouldn't she already be
mine..
I feel like.. I shouldn't even say what I feel
Because it'll be too much
I've literally loved her since the day I met her

I felt so comfortable like I was home..
I've never felt that way about anyone in my
entire life
It's just her
It's always been her
I can't believe she even wants me back..
It's hard to believe most days
When she says something sweet to me it still
surprises me and makes my entire day
Because the thought of her loving me..
Is something I never saw coming
Like I don't deserve her
She deserves the entire world and I'm just
damaged
I know I could love her harder than most
But maybe that's not what she needs
So I back off
But I just want to explode some days
I want to tell her how amazing and loved she is
every single minute of the day..
I can't sleep when I haven't spent any time with
her because I crave her in every way
I miss her so much
It never stops
Make it stop..
I just want her next to me
So I can breathe again
But she doesn't feel the same
She doesn't love me as hard

She treats me amazing. Better than anyone ever
has..
But she doesn't love me like I love her
Because if she did.. she would be here
And I don't blame her for that
It's not her fault
Feelings are valid and hers are the most
important in the world to me
I just want her to be happy
But I want her to be with me
Because I'm afraid that's the only time I'm truly
happy
I know I can make myself happy and I do..
But I'm my best self when she's around..
I can't even walk away even if I should..
Because a world without her is dark
It's not even worth living in

7 Times

She say she in love with me
He said do you love me
He just wants a hug, squeeze
She want that ice cream, freeze
She just wanna fuck (me)
Mother I'd like to fuck? Please
She already been on her knees
I already been in between
She just wanna ride, freak
30 seconds done, weak
Mama got a secret, link
Baby walk on tiptoes, sneak
She just wanna rub
Eyes on us don't touch
Babe come here, don't rush
Keep it between us, hush
Whisper in my ear (fuck)
Reply to your hubs (bruh 😕)
Who comin above huh?
Liars wanna judge ya
Got me out here wondering
Wanderlust found me underneath
Switch up keep on stirring
Pot or kettle? We burnin 🔥
Speak her love language (mi amor)

Making love in the dark (paramour)
Hit the backboard she want more
Hit the baseboard now home run(score)
Bed ain't close hit the deck (floor)
Had to come in the back (door)
Went from bestfriend to baby (girl)
Keep it explicit you switched up illicit
Mouthy then moanin while I tongue kiss it
Hit a wall I push her up against it
Hit it but can't seem to quit it
Win or lose some I still win
Might not be daddy I still get it in
7 times and deadly (father I sin)

I'm Sorry

It's funny
People say I speak so eloquently
Might have all the right words but claimin
you're mine doesn't seem fair to me
Look at yourself through my eyes so you can see
what I see

It's your smile for me
First time I saw it made me feel something
Not sure if you'll stay but I don't want you to
leave..
Feeling like you're genuine but it's hard for me
to believe

Beginning is always the same
Fall in love, talk about taking my last name
Middle of the night it's only you that I tame
Leave me like the rest and I'll take the blame

You asked me if I could hurt you
I wanted to say no but that wouldn't be true
But I think about my future and you're the only
view
Long distance gets hard but I want to see this
through

My girl, soon to be fiancé and my future wife
You must be a dream because this isn't real life
So many walls up but you're determined to take them down
I've got memories that haunt me all over this town

Realized my life is nothing but a sad story
Tryna love you in all the right ways but I fuck up and I'm sorry
Confused cause with you I don't even worry
Everyone's been guilty, don't put me on the jury

Oh.. How She Spins

Remember when you used to joke that you
didn't have a mom
She was more like a friend that was back and
forth you had no choice but to play along
Guess I never learned the difference between
right and wrong
What's wrong to you feels normal to me I know
I'll never belong
Just like that girl who doesn't belong to me,
that's the vibe I stay on
We sing to the best parts and then skip to the
next song
Some say it's a game but to me doesn't feel like
playing
Words not matching actions just means I didn't
understand what you were saying
We'll try again once you rephrase it
The tears don't fall because it's a sunny day,
mom told me to save it
I saved them for a rainy day wanted a hug but
she wouldn't embrace it
Back to fake happy dancing alone in the rain,
my play pretend
Call it what you want but titles stand for nothing
in the end

Consistency is a lie in the mind of a little girl
who never stayed on a priority list
You love me today I'm busy preparing for
tomorrow when I'm nothing again
See this is how I'm still okay when your big
smile fades to a simple grin
I'm grateful for the grin it means you're still
here I'm not disappearing into my head again
She said she wanted to marry me suddenly I'm 5
years old in my dress playing pretend
We dance in the rain together, my heart is finally
on the mend
Promised me forever but she'll break it so I must
bend
Save the dates read "one day" with all these
words I'll type but never feel safe enough to
send
I smile at the thought I'm no longer alone, she's
holding me close
Take off the dress take off the smile I'm only
allowed to grin
It's time to walk away now but oh.. how she
spins 🖤

Comfort In the Chaos

It's dangerous
Feeling comfortable in the chaos
Every new friend is just another loss
Thought you could play games, take a seat I'm
the boss
Fake as your smile, go grab some floss

Brag about your new clothes but can't pay your
rent
I drew the blueprint you just throwing down
cement
Took my car out for a spin then lied to me bout
the dent
Forget the small talk today, I gotta vent

Is this fake love again or the real deal?
Got a cute girl they all tryna steal
Close friends being shady are you forreal
Your fate? It's time to seal

Feeling unsafe when things are out of my
control
Should probably slow down but that's not how I
roll

Thought you had me locked down? I got out on parole
Callin you baby doll whole time you're a troll

High up in the sky my ears starting to pop
Ride the roller coaster up and down just to feel the drop
Popped another addy, shit maybe I should stop
Moving to Oklahoma? That's not soda it's a pop

We all have our vices don't matter what it cost
Took the road less traveled now I'm just fucking lost
Processing shit by myself cause I ain't a snitch
Big top energy but you actually a switch
Claimin she's your girl but always someone else's bitch
Popped a perc to numb the pain now it's makin me itch

Lost my family, weight and sanity in the span of a year
Vision went blurry but it's starting to clear
Riding pretty in my passenger seat but thinking maybe you should steer
Man up and treat her right or go grab another beer

Block me so you don't have to face me
Go ahead sum me up to somebody you'll never
be
Post pics of this perfect couple for the world to
see
Behind closed doors it's nothing but anxiety

Everybody's got an opinion but nobody's got my
back
Maybe she overdosed on heroin fentanyl or
crack
Head between my knees having a panic attack
The walls closed in and faded to black

If I disappeared would I ever be found?
Woke up in a hospital bed with nobody around
Feeling abandoned and alone, get me back on
solid ground
Praying someone would hear me but nobody
made a sound

Let me talk to the assholes who put the "I" in
team
Give you my support but silently wanting to
scream
Not even mad at you baby I'm just lettin off
steam
Hoping we wake up one day and this is all just a
dream..

Through My Eyes

Do everything with passion
My intensity is the reason you're attracted
Showed you everything that your person was
lackin
Shouldn't ask me to stay but I've got you
distracted

Beautiful smile but sadness in her eyes
With me it's only see you laters, never goodbyes
Not your girl but I'll be yours tonight
Get lost in my eyes, now you're ready for blue
skies

See I believe everything happens for a reason
I could live in this moment forever, you think
I'm only here for a season
Loving you, giving you something to believe in
Two stepping on my heart, secretly dancing with
my demons

Make you feel safe, tell me every little detail
Block my number and leave me, I'm sending
you an email
Love makes you blind, I learned to read in
braille
Yeah you stole my heart but I posted your bail

Writing you poems so you'll soak up every line
Talking to you all day, no sleep but I'm fine
Got you in your feelings after that dark horse
wine
Life gets easier and you wish that you were mine

Want me but don't need me, I'm yours to keep
Look at me like a snack, ima marshmallow peep
🐦
Show me you'll ride or die, I'm buying us a jeep
Lost your faith in humanity, I'll teach you how
to leap

Anything you want your wish is my command
Need a road trip or an adventure, I'm dropping a
grand
Matching tattoos, writing our names in the sand
Think you're falling for me, I'll move over
before you land

Feet on solid ground confused and alone, but
you still stand
See you weren't falling for me, I was holding
your hand
Falling in love with life and yourself, only thing
I had planned
Made you see yourself through my eyes, they'll
never steal your fire again 🔥 🖤

Built Different

Here's the difference between you and me
Most of y'all wishin things were different,
readin fairytales wondering why you can't be
like them
Most of y'all so bored just scrolling lookin for
entertainment
Most of y'all so miserable you wanna take a
good thing and try to break it
What's understood doesn't have to be announced
so I don't say shit
You tryna convince the world you're happy or
just yourself? Think about it
Stay together because you made a promise
But you having convos with your besties that are
way more honest
Situation ain't resolved but he tellin you to drop
it
Always so negative why you can't get off the
topic?
No accountability so you stop makin comments
Ups and downs? This ain't a ride, get off it
Signed a paper now you stuck forever, where's
the logic?
Yeah that's your person but they stopped tryna
win you

Stopped puttin in the work they don't even finish you
Lost your self worth and your motivation the mirror don't even recognize you
Yeah you fucked up he fucked up too
Gotta forgive him cause he forgave you, time for round 72
It's okay cause the back and forth is what you're used to
Everyone's got shit they gotta work through
How you still in love when the effort stopped being mutual
I don't come with a rule book, don't sign on no dotted lines
Claimin people like property, I signed so she's mine ?
Drop the label and see what happens
Set someone free they find pieces of themselves they were lacking
Didn't realize you molded yourself to make him happy
You hid the parts that he didn't like and threw away the key
Every decision affects "we" but what would you choose if it only affected "me"
What if he chooses somebody else? Then I guess you been livin in a fantasy
You're here because you're mine not because you want to be

That's the kinda crap I don't want or need
Doing what makes you happy is a different kind
of free
Nobody keeping tabs like who you with or
where you be
I can do life with my girl and still live my life
for me
If the label changes anything then she never
wanted me for me
Most people want control want somebody they
can keep
Most people got possession and call it love, keep
the superficial, I want deep
Most people want to see the top of the mountain
but give up once the climb is too steep
Facebook posts are just what they want people
to see
Behind closed doors it's just another bad story
Don't get comfortable with me
I'm only doing life with you if you adding to my
peace
Love me as I am or watch me when I leave
Honesty and respect is the only real key
I want you to love me but only if you're free
Changing yourself only causes resentment you'll
see
You gotta love yourself more than you love me
Be selfish with your time because people are
greedy

I promise you need you more than you need me
Yes I'm a priority but first you need to sleep
You need to eat you need to breathe
Train your mind to be strong instead of close
minded and weak
Don't let anyone make you feel like you're
underneath
I made it to the top of the mountain, tell me how
far can you reach?
Most people ain't tryna listen they just wanna
preach
Mama washed my mouth with soap for tellin
lies, I'm the remix, I use bleach
Better watch your tone before you speak
Been told I'm unapproachable best comment I
ever received
If that's the case then why you still approaching
me
Drop another negative comment, that make you
feel better than me?
Set in your ways and believe everything you
read
Flip the table or stop complaining
What you are is what you'll always be
Gossip behind my back but switch up when it's
just you and me
Wish you could speak your mind but you scared
and retreat
What would people think if they saw the real me

What if they disown me
What if I get lonely
What if I stay trapped in this mindset and never
see the grown me
What if this don't feel like home because I can't
make a home in me
What if I keep doubting love cause I doubt my
own love for me
Negative thoughts on repeat not good enough
I'm ugly
Hiding parts of myself that others didn't want to
see
Playin it safe is like a nightmare but you're
awake
Never take the chance don't complain to me
when it's too late
Wake up everyday and determine your own fate
Leave it up to the liars and the fakes
Yeah their posts look happy and life is great
Social media is quiet when they ain't doin okay
Everyone's "fine" why they lyin in bed wide
awake?
Keep telling yourself tomorrow is a new day
Wake up same mindset, same outcome, same
mistakes

Here's the difference between you and me
I think before I speak and keep it lowkey

I watch and observe because snakes slither
slowly
I'm confident being me so I don't get lonely
Most people too scared to try something new
Most people too scared to admit that they even
want to
If it's not trending, it's not normal if it's not what
the majority of people do
I make people uncomfortable by doing what
they don't do
Somebody on the mountain now they wanna
climb it too
Snakes gettin uncomfortable once they can't
reach, sayin it's too steep you'll never make it
through
They sayin you changed nah they just never
knew the real you
Brave girl on the mountain makin you see
something new
If she can do it then you can too
Might be a hard climb but damn.. it's a beautiful
view 😍

RIP

Hero left too soon, guess I'm stuck lookin up to
villains
No one coming to save you, take this noose hang
it to the ceilin
"Might need therapy, you're crying again"
RIP to who I could've been

Gunshots and loss, two different heads
Addiction and depression run deep, you're fine
just take these meds
Damned if I do and damned if I don't
Show me some empathy, you won't

Put me down then love me, it's a constant chase
Type it out, hit send, you never wanted to see my
face
Look me in the eyes, did you notice they're
pretty and blue
Convince me I'll never be good enough, (wait is
that true?)

Speaking my mind so now I'm just bipolar and
crazy
Raising little siblings cause both parents gettin
lazy
One second, one shot to start a cycle of trauma
 "That's not your story to tell, you just want
drama"

Am I invisible or just a spoiled brat?
Pop my mouth til I'm quiet, teachers wondering
why I don't talk back
Kids aren't worth living for, you gave up on life
"Marry someone like your mama" now I gotta
save my wife

Punished for showing emotion, pretend I'm not
even phased
I can hide every feeling and thought now, you'd
be so amazed
Used to be too little to beat you at this game
Playing back now since I'm grown, does that
mean we're the same?…

Row Row Row

Thought you were next to me must've been a
shadow
Found somebody new I ain't even mad tho
Wishing on a dandelion count to three then blow
Boat filled up with water you better row row
row

Sticks and stones ain't breaking my bones but
words are startin to hurt
Pink really isn't my color but man I miss that
shirt
Dinner dates aren't my thing I like to start with
dessert
Forever lasted a year, just another lesson learned

Wishing I knew my grandma now that I'm older
Undiagnosed they called her crazy, bipolar
Hard to love a person who always gives a cold
shoulder
Gun to the head no more options, they broke her
💔

What if they loved her instead of calling her
crazy

Think somebody has your back, turn around
they acting shady
Picked the wrong one today if you tryna play me
Grandma passed the crazy down, sorry you
couldn't phase me

One two buckle my shoe
So much shit I been through
Why do good people always get screwed
Tryna leave the past in the rear view

Silver linings is what she called them
It's the orange coming up over the horizon
It's that late night drive with your person just
vibin
It's finding the right timing when you want it
right then

A surprise visit when you least expect it Making
someone smile when their day has been hectic
Realizing that break up was actually a blessing
Someone noticing your hard work when you
never get the credit

Three four better lock that door
One minute you fine next minute you're on the
floor
Running errands ain't even fun it's just another
chore

Going through the motions I can't do this
anymore

Trapped inside my mind but not even afraid
Don't believe in fear, always open to change
Lately I feel nothing and it's startin to feel
strange
Mighta been your target but I'm way outta your
range

Gotta be more to life than just eat sleep exist
Used to love the rain now I'm settlin for mist
Saw a shooting star didn't even make a wish
You fine without me now, don't act like I'll be
missed 🖤

Pretty Rose

"Plant a seed"
Pretty rose
"Take a chill pill"
You froze
"Not original"
One of those
"Fake a smile"
No more tone
"Low on cash"
Get a loan
"Love you much"
Monotone
"Want me back"
Ready go

Big bright eyes
New nickname Goldie
A fish behind the glass
They just stare at me
Manic again
Forgot to start therapy
5 minutes later you ready to marry me
You think you can save me
These thoughts they been scarin me
Don't want you to fix me

Maybe just sit with me
Eskimo sisters
Heard you share chicks with me
Want that in writing
You settle for digitally
No control C
This shit is real to me
These pills give no thrills to me
Don't even feel real to me
Fading away
Just feelin numb
Be more aggressive
Make me feel sum'n
Don't want you to go
Need you to run
Gotta be faster
Back on the hunt
Grab him a 30
He want those in cans
Stay on that weak shit
I got mine in grams
Milli Vanilli
I meant milligrams
Yeah I can drive
Don't ask me to stand
Skip the cliff notes
Summarize I got banned
Fucked up the numbers
Cancel my plans

Still falling for her
Call ya when I land
Let go of her hand
She said hold on tighter
Saw the end of existence
Or my future got brighter
Silver linings ain't silver
Just a big white liar
You calling him Frodo
I'm baggin the shire
Hit that new low low
Should be on my old dose
You wanted the choice
Guess this what you chose

"6 foot distance"
Above ground or below?
"Figure it out love"
Either way you're alone

Eye to Eye

Living in a fairytale
Nah
It's a fable
Want me to eat?
Show me the table
Holding all the cards
Went from toxic to stable
Plumerias are pretty
Happiness on their label
Fine print says toxic
Cross out happy
I'm not able

See no evil comes first
Close your eyes
Less it hurts
Hear no evil comes second
Water gun
Make it squirt
Speak no evil comes third
Heart on your sleeve
Shrink the shirt

Add the evil
Physical touch

Flip to the backside
Now in reverse

Told you I'm done
Choose what to see
Three wise monkeys
Here's your bedtime story

Can't speak
Water damage
Hold up
Grab the rice

Can't hear
Make it louder
I slipped in
Black ice

Can't see
Feel for me
Done again
Three blind mice

Eye to eye
Look closely
You know the real me
What I made you believe
Legends are made up
Interesting to read

Fantasy turned reality
I'm not what you need

47

Back and Forth

One second you're comfortable
Next second running away
Lay in bed at night
Go over every single thing I did today
Did I reveal too much
Did I feel too much
Was I wrong to reach for your touch
They're not worth your tears
Straighten your shoulders
Walk in like you own the place
Don't let them see you frown
People actin like they're above you
See those notches? Knock them down
Show them they can't hurt you
Make sure nobody fucks with you
Emotion is weakness
Comfort is unattainable
Love is manipulation
I take care of you, better show you're grateful
Show me you don't care
Next lesson rage, get hateful
I have a thing for lists
Keeps my thoughts organized
The list of people I trust
You might be surprised

Got a few ride or dies
But my name didn't make the cut
Cause see I want trust but I know I've told lies
They told me it was wrong to like girls and not
guys
Once I get comfortable I feel compromised
If sky is the limit, I limit the skies
Give you endless chances you get so many tries
But me fuck up once and I'm out of your life
I do it to myself
Can't even blame you
It's in my DNA
Comfort ain't something I do
Comfort means still I'm always searching for
more
Once you find peace in me, that's when my
mind goes to war
Love isn't comfortable
Why stop when there's more
I could be better
Work harder
Show you I can be someone you adore
Get comfortable with my actions
I'm back to being invisible
I could do this by myself and not have to worry
about what I did to you
See you might hurt me but it's my actions that
triggered you
I've always took the blame

Demons don't stop til they finish you
Broken and empty with no love to give
How can I give something without knowing
what it is
What happens if I give in
What if I added my name to the list
What if I trusted in myself and eventually in us
What if I gave you all of me and it still wasn't
enough
Then you'd prove my theory to be true
I guess I've got nothing to lose
But with nothing to lose there's nothing to give
Winning me isn't the prize
Learning to love yourself through my eyes
Once you realize there's no limits, just skies
You won't settle for the nothing that I had to
give

Less Lover, More Fighter

Tryna identify my triggers before it's too late,
I'm a goner
Not piglet not tigger just an Eeyore sad loner
Still I'm always here catch your tears on my
shoulder
Maybe everything will make sense once I'm
older
Told my psychiatrist I have trouble paying
attention
Squirrel brain like an off the track train
Like Puff the Magic Dragon was my fav song in
2nd grade
Say whatever to get my way, damn somebody
fucked me up in the brain
They ask me "who do you lean on"
Myself.. but it rarely goes well
I sleep next to my girl at peace be still
Wake up hit my vape caffeinate pop another pill
Addicted got the prescription
I could stop feel the pain but then I don't want to
be alive/existing
My song lyrics aren't even half of what I
actually feel
The lights flicker around me something spiritual
is near

Maybe I'm the ghost half alive don't even
realize that I'm not real
No that post wasn't about you
Take it personal cause that's what you do
If the shoe fits lace that bitch up and..
throw it back in the closet
Next to those expensive hardly worn doc
martens
Don't need reminders that I lost another person
Lack of communication just makes me nauseous
If I tie your shoelaces I always double knot them
Lock n Deadbolt the front door keepin you safe
is my only option
Look I'm done tryna match your energy
Save the apology never cared what you did to
me
They say this too shall pass, yeah like a stone in
my kidney
Even when I'm alone always feel like
somebody's watching
Constantly on high alert I take extra precautions
Probably never trust another soul if I'm being
honest
Sometimes feels like I'm not making any
progress
Gotta stay numb to this feeling, you still haunt
my subconscious
I wake up screaming wish my brain had an off
switch

I guess I'm good at sharing because
Anything that was ever fully mine always turned
out temporary
My favorite number was always 8 turn it
sideways now it's forever/infinity
Feels out of reach/impossible but I thrive on the
possibility..
Keep an open mind whatever situation I'm
thrown in
Never mine for the keeping I'm just grateful for
what I'm given
It never mattered how small or how little
Sometimes it's the smallest things that make the
biggest difference
Look I don't have regrets
And I don't know what's next
But I can solve any problem just give me a sec
Your tears don't phase me while I put you in
check
If you hurt me on purpose that's a RIP friendship
Funeral in my head said you buried/gone/dead
One day might be toxic next day I'm healing
Like my weight it fluctuates
Like the dose gets higher when I'm in my
feelings
Like I'll always love you but only from a
distance
And if you need an ear I'll listen
But if you got problems then let me help fix em

Like I'll be polite until you disrespect one of
these fools I sit with
Overprotective don't try to filter now I'm just
here to hurt feelings
Not gonna say sorry whenever I'm not
Complex I don't fit in anyone's box
Don't follow crowds cause one size does not fit
all
I'm firm and strong the reviews they weren't
wrong
If you stay by my side you might get to see my
soft
Keeping the peace that's never been me
Try to use my words against me I'll say them
louder, repeat
Stay behind your screen type out a subtweet
Might be a lot of things but I ain't never been
weak
Don't even flinch when I watch scary movies
Diagnosed BPD I promise you always got me
Or Charlie with the multiple personalities. Go
watch Hide and Seek
Little bit of everything but no diagnosis
Genetics they pester me first born daughter has
to learn first
Alzheimer's might lose my mind
Suicide gun to the head might be bipolar
Colon cancer slow killer skin turning yellow
Ignore my text ima pop up sayin "hello"

It's the boogeyman or the slender man night
terrors
Say it 3 times in the dark "Bloody Mary"
Ghosts and monsters they never scared me
It's the cold dead eyes in the mirror staring back
at me
I'm fine with surprises let's pull the mattress out
the box
Let's be happy with what we had even if it stays
lost
But..
Take away the magic that lady gets cut in half
with a chainsaw?!
You can "abracadabra" to the disappearing hat
but can't deny that Jill sometimes chooses to be
Jack
People don't have to understand you, see
common sense is something they always lacked
Not being pessimistic I mean facts are just facts
But your worth still getting tossed and that
magic hat isn't bringing it back
Cut out the negative energy leave the mistakes in
the past
Sometimes bossy, They call me boss, I'll take
my 7 million in cash 🤪
If I had a dollar for every time you made me
laugh
I'd buy a fancy ass mattress throw the old one
with old memories in the trash

See I don't give a fuck what you think about me
Keep followin the crowd whatever you want to
believe in
This hasn't been my season had no one to lean
on
Might pop up on your "for you" page but
don't bother clicking that heart once I'm finally
trending
Most people only want you when you winning
Bunch of robots with no original thoughts
I said "hey siri" to Alexa now she pissed off
Love me or love me not
Let the petals fall, still finding where I belong
You wanna shit talk go sit by my mom
Don't do small minds and I'll skip the small talk
Roses tattooed on like my confidence, and I hear
you can't scrub that shit off
✌

Call me a bitch watch you downgrade to bro
Ignore my calls must be talkin to that other ho
60 hour weeks collect $200
You like playin games I brought monopoly,
looks like I passed go 😆
I leveled up to somebody you'll never know
Not gonna filter my thoughts take me off
speakerphone
Not gonna poly your amorous been there done
that before

That one on one hit different I only want you
alone
Less lover, more fighter
I'll always sit with you in the dark til your future
gets brighter
Why do I always love the liars
Just an earth sign forever attracted to fire

I Do Matter

I'm the bread winner you colonel mustard like
get a clue
That bad attitude contagious like miss Peacock
spread the bird flu
He she they them wait.. who the fuck is you?
Gay bi wavy straight that Christian chicken still
taste the same
"I'm only here for the sauce" compliments of
chick fil a
To go/curbside, only eat the fries
Tolerance is way too high
Stomach empty pretty blue bloodshot eyes
What sustains me when there's nothing inside
Who's there with a shoulder when I need to cry
Hate to admit we all need help sometimes
If it comes down to him or me, pick the other
guy
My loyalty unmatched see I ride or die
I'm winning this race, try to convince me
otherwise
Oh you got a new number, now I gotta block it
twice
Workin on that psych degree more than 1
personality
Naughty by the end of the day I might be nice

I match energy better play ya cards right
Same blood when we bleed 💧
You didn't have to hurt me
No we not family
I ain't got no beef
No we not enemies
You put me underneath
I got different beliefs
Never believed in me
Gotta stay out your reach
I'm no better than you
But tomorrow ima be a better me
Unclenching my fists relearn how to breathe
2nd grade 750 books only took 28 days to read
3rd grade learning 6th grade words got picked
for the spelling bee
4th grade perfecting my magic tricks see there's
real then there's make believe
If you don't believe in the magic maybe you
could believe in yourself..
Or even in me
Another win another attempt to make you see
Alone in my room watching Disney be the only
time I see any kind of Proud Family
Baby steps but I'm puttin in the work
I still believe in magic and fixing the hurt
We're all a little broken but I promise I'll leave
you better than you were

No baby girl you not in love with me you just
finally feel seen feel heard
Finding my way helping others find their worth
28 years on this Earth
Biggest lesson think I finally learned
I do matter and what's crazy is… I have since
birth

Full Moon Kinda Night

Not sure what feelings are normal
Am I angry or just hormonal?
Do I need these depression meds or a new
situation
Always been good at math, didn't have a proper
example but still expected to solve every
equation
I can tell you the correct answer but my method
wasn't step by step so I can't really explain it
"Show your work" I'll turn in a blank page then
My mind is all over the place you wouldn't
understand my directionally challenged brain
Don't believe in right or wrong ways
Some people do things differently some people
are afraid so they play it safe
Soon as I'm back on track everything goes up in
flames
Burned every bridge following GPS to heavens
gate
Storms rolling in might cause some delays
Might make some more mistakes but that's okay
Fetal position holding my shoulders little girl
trapped alone and caged
Door is unlocked doesn't mean that I can run
away

I know you'll still paint the picture that way
I'm insane fucked in the brain staying stuck in
this space
I did this to myself I never tried to escape
Had nowhere to run, but see I didn't choose to
stay
Smiling on the outside no matter what I feel that
day
That confidence in your tone doesn't make your
feelings fact
Just turned around to feel another stab in the
back
My feelings said out loud now you're personally
attacked
Got you feelin bad for your behavior
Got me saying sorry for pointing out where you
lack
Its me and you against the problem but you
never seem to get that
You take it to heart and up goes your guard
I'm the one who's hurt but my words in between
us I'd like to take back
Bad posture had to make myself smaller
Seeing eye to eye was never an option,
Just a walking reminder of everything you never
had
See
We can't turn words to actions when there's no
accountability for how you act

How I feel is overwhelming on the defense you
always react
Always walking away you don't gotta be like
that
Are we talking or arguing?
Is this healthy or bad?
These red flags feel normal when they're all I've
ever had
So confused on what to do wish I could ask dad
The grass is green where you choose to water it,
forget having any colored flags
Nothing but lies, gaslight me until I'm color
blind
Nothing feels normal when wrong feels right
I try to be good they still walk out my life
Starting to wonder why I even try
I finally leave my cage
They all cheer, call me brave
Little do they know
The trap was always in my mind
I have to lock the door now..
It's only safe when I'm inside

I look to the sky and wish for the rain
It's funny my dad would shush me because I'd
always get my way
See I don't wait for sunshine to go outside and
play

I don't hope for the best I don't hide the pain
I throw my hands in the air and I dance anyway
"I CALL THAT FAVOR" my mom would laugh
and say
She took me outside
Had to show me the night sky
We may never see eye to eye
But I thought you should know..
I forgave you a long time ago
You did the best you could, gave me something
to look up to
My heart stays full, just like those nights we
watched the moon
Those nights I'm still outside just to see the
pretty view
I smile then wonder what it must feel like to be
you
Shit gets real suddenly I'm fighting back tears
Sometimes it hits me out of nowhere
I want to run I don't want to be here
I want my mom, nah fuck that I want to
disappear
I'm here I'm there nobody knows nobody cares
I'm fine, I'm smiling, but did you notice the
moon isn't as bright?
Did you notice I wait around for full moons so
you'll take me back outside
I wonder if you ever loved me

I wonder if I'm good enough, then I learned to
stop asking you
Your mom pulled the trigger but that bullet left a
hole inside you too
You walk around empty and don't know what to
do
That betrayal leaves a scar that doesn't fully heal
Our traumas aren't the same but both very real
Physically abandoned never found your worth
Emotionally abused my life has been a lie since
birth
I wish you never had me
Wish I didn't remind you of that pain, of her
I'm truly sorry for hurting you, I apologize over
and over (for what it's worth)
I wonder what it's like on Saturn I don't belong
on this earth
Not to compare our traumas but you were better
off that your mom died
I often wonder why I'm alone when my
Mom is still alive
No filter I say what's on my mind
You don't have to like me or talk to me that's
fine
Can't hurt my feelings when I'm always fine
Can't handle fake smiles, small talk
The pain in my back gotta push then pop
Deliver the food, snap a pic, speed off
No tip when we in the ghetto

Should probably flinch more at the gun shots
Just a normal day with my overthinking thoughts
More night terrors hidden trauma, subconscious
Full moon is bright shadows to light
I wonder if I'll be a good mom
I wonder how I'll react when I get things wrong
What if it feels wrong to hold her when she cries
What if my love is never enough what if she
feels the same way that I do inside
What if she has your eyes and the hurt
overpowers all the love I had inside
What if you had answered my questions and I
wasn't trapped in constant fight or flight
What if my muscles stopped hurting and I
finally realized
Take a deep breath while you can nobody makes
it out alive
We can dwell on the negative or focus on
something bright
It's okay you tried
I probably won't get to say goodbye
The playing field is even the day that you die
I don't have to compete or feel weak when I cry
I don't have to make you proud and fuck I'm
exhausted from trying
Wait until you see your trauma was only an
excuse to never try
Wait until you watch me get back on my feet
Stare in disbelief

I'd pay money to see
I'm nothing like your mom. And you never
loved me
But I wonder sometimes if you wonder about me
When we're both outside
Full moon kinda night
Waiting and watching underneath the same sky

Two Little Girls

I prayed for safety, something more than just a
roof
I prayed to be healthy now I take medicine
before I can eat any food
Crying alone just a little girl in my room
"Mommy I'm out of bed again come spank me"
begged for attention since I was two
I prayed over and over that tomorrow I'd be
good enough for you
They told me to have faith but it's the end of
another day and I said goodnight to the moon
You made me act out and told me I was bad
Now that I'm older I'm actually kinda glad
You brought out this love in me that nobody can
match or outdo
See I stopped praying for myself, what good did
that do
I'm always going to be bad so let me switch up
this view
I once thought you were an Angel but now I see
you've fallen too
Your mom took her own life it wasn't your fault
there was nothing you could do
I write like her, look like her, she didn't just take
one life away she took two

I picture you as a little girl crying alone in your
room
I'm too much like her always wrong in your
eyes no matter what I say or do
But there's always been a difference and here's a
few

Your little girl prayed for Satan and I pray for
you

www.ingramcontent.com/pod-product-compliance
Lightning Source LLC
LaVergne TN
LVHW021212200726

843509LV00012B/1425